YOU CAN

IF YOU THINK YOU CAN

REBOUND FROM ADVERSITY
AND FOLLOW YOUR DREAMS

SIMPLE STRATEGIES TO ACHIEVE
SUCCESS AND HAPPINESS IN YOUR LIFE

By Larry P. Johnson, M.A., PHR

Copyright © 2008 Larry P. Johnson
All rights reserved.

ISBN: 1-4392-1331-3
ISBN-13: 9781439213315

Visit www.booksurge.com to order additional copies.

YOU CAN

IF YOU THINK YOU CAN

ABOUT THE AUTHOR

Larry P. Johnson is a graduate of Northwestern University's School of Speech, in Evanston, Illinois. He earned his Master's in Economics & Latin American Studies, from La Universidad de las Americas in Mexico City.

His professional background includes:
- 21 years as a Human Resources manager with SBC/AT&T Communications. He is accredited as a Personnel Specialist by the National Personnel Accreditation Institute.
- 22 years as a radio and television broadcaster in Mexico City, Chicago and San Antonio. He broadcast the 1968 Olympics in Mexico City, the 1969 Apollo 11 "Lunar Landing", and was the first blind American newscaster on Mexican television.
- 28 years as a motivational speaker and workshop presenter. He is a dynamic international keynote speaker and workshop presenter, having presented for audiences at conferences and conventions, for community and civic organizations, colleges, government agencies and private corporations in Mexico, Japan and the United States.

He is the author of Mexico By Touch: True Life Experiences of a Blind American Deejay, an account of his adventures and misadventures living and working in Mexico for 17 years and "Relax And Live," a professionally narrated guided relaxation exercise recorded on CD.

Recognizing that success and happiness are more attainable when people learn how to rebound from failure and adversity and that our "dream goals" can be achieved if we follow a step-by-step approach, Larry developed a dynamic, interactive training seminar that he has been conducting for the past seven years for audiences of disadvantaged youth, single moms, displaced workers, dispirited employees, and other adults with low self-esteem and poor self-confidence. This book is the outgrowth of those seminars.

COMMENTS RECEIVED FROM WORKSHOP PARTICIPANTS

Randolph Air Force Base - Administrative Staff

"It was an inspiration." "It reinforced positive thinking."

"I noticed the change in everyone from day one, to the second day."

El Paso Community College – Administrative Staff

"Inspiring and motivational." "Excellent workshop, very beneficial."

"I learned how to organize my thoughts and goals."

"Very good points and very refreshing."

Randolph-Brooks Federal Credit Union, Management & Staff

"Found it very useful. Learned a lot about improving my self-esteem."

"I liked the inspiring stories, the Affirmation and the Compliment Circle."

"I learned that other people have the same worries and problems as I do. It was great."

Texas Workforce Center – Classes of Displaced Workers

"The workshop was great. It showed me how to be a good person and how to reach my goals."

"It brought me encouragement." "It helped give me a new outlook toward my goal and toward my unemployment."

"Showed me a lot about myself. Thank you with all my heart."

Texas Dept. of Rehabilitation - (Staff Training)

"The words and the examples all seemed to have been directed to me."

"I learned important principles to be applied in various areas of my life."

"I liked the enlightening uplifting feeling I had during the presentation, the encouragement and being able to look at myself in a positive manner."

"I liked being able to dream and the specificness as to how to get it done."

Chris Cole Rehabilitation Center – Client Class

"I learned to laugh and accept myself and to accept failure."

"I can now look at myself in a positive way."

"After listening to the presentation my self-esteem became very high."

"Did is a word of achievement
Won't is a word of defeat
Might is a word of bereavement
Can't is a word of defeat
Ought is a word of duty
Try is a word each hour
Will is a word of beauty
Can is a word of power."

Gerard Hargraves

"What you choose today will ripple throughout a thousand tomorrows."

— Dr. Deepak Chopra, Chairman and co-Founder of the Chopra Center for Wellbeing in Carlsbad, California. Acknowledged as one of the world's greatest leaders in the field of mind body medicine.

TO MY CHILDREN, MY CHILDREN'S CHILDREN AND TO THE WHOLE HUMAN RACE:

KNOWLEDGE IS THE LAMP THAT LIGHTS OUR hopes and possibilities AND GIVES US THE POWER TO pursue OUR DREAMS.

LPJ

YOU CAN
If You Think You Can

INTRODUCTION

Do you feel life has given you nothing but lemons?
Are you discouraged, disappointed and dejected?
Have you given up on your dreams?
Then, this book is for you.

Personal rejection, disappointments or temporary failures can often damage our self-confidence and self-esteem.

Not long ago, I was in the supermarket waiting in the check-out line with just a couple of items I'd purchased. As it turned out the customer ahead of me was a friend of the cashier. They began a very animated conversation about their boyfriends and last Saturday night's dates. After waiting a couple of minutes, I became impatient. Turning to the cashier, I said: "Would you mind checking me out?" Glancing at me quickly she replied: "I already have, and you're too old."

That could have been a devastating blow to my self-esteem, but I just smiled, flattered that she even considered me as a prospect.

Some people are able to take rejection, disappointment and failure right in stride, while others are devastated by it. Why is this?

Self-esteem—feeling worthy and able to meet life's challenges—is as essential as the air we breathe and just as intangible. It can impact our job, happiness, health, and our relationships with others.

The development of healthy self-esteem and self-confidence enables a person to respond and adapt to the demands of life in a confident manner, to deal with adversity and to follow their dreams. The ability to be resilient—able to bounce back from disappointment, rejection or a temporary setback—is the key to building and maintaining our self-esteem and achieving success and happiness.

Stress in our lives, whether caused by family problems, illness, the death of a loved one, the loss of a job, divorce, or a financial setback can greatly deplete our reserves of self-confidence and self-esteem. The good news is that we can rebuild it.

OBJECTIVES:
This book is divided into two parts:
1. How to rebound from adversity and
2. How to fulfill your dreams

In Part One, we will emphasize three important principles:
1. Low self-esteem negatively impacts personal health, job performance and our relationships with others.
2. There are simple, effective strategies that can be used to regain self-esteem and rebound from adversity and temporary setbacks.
3. Having high self-esteem and a positive mental attitude are the keys to success and happiness.

Through these pages you will learn how to be resilient ... to rebound from adversity, disappointments and temporary failure. We will identify those factors that contribute to high and low self-esteem, help you understand your limiting beliefs and behaviors, and outline steps you can take to make a positive change.

In Part Two, we will invite you to choose your Dream Goals—those things you most wish to achieve—lose weight, find a new job, quit smoking, buy a house, finish college, change your life. Then we are going to show you how to transform those Dream Goals into reality. And, if you are patient enough, committed enough and willing to sacrifice enough, I assure you that you can and will attain your Dream Goals.

PART 1: REBOUNDING FROM ADVERSITY

SELF-RATING EXERCISE

How are you feeling right now about yourself? How would you rate your self-esteem? On the Self-Rating Exercise sheet appearing on the following page, rate yourself on a scale of 1 to 10, with 1 indicating very low self-esteem and 10 indicating having very high self-esteem.

Be honest with yourself. You don't have to show your rating to anyone, and you will be asked to rate yourself several times more as you read through this book. A rating of 1 or 10 is most unlikely for anyone.

Write the date and time next to your rating. If you feel concerned because your rating seems a bit low, don't worry. The good news is that self-esteem can be regained and increased. Our feelings of self-esteem and self-confidence are not constant. They ebb and flow like the ocean tide. They are influenced by many factors. We'll talk about some of those factors in the following pages.

SELF-ESTEEM RATING EXERCISE

SCORE YOURSELF ON A SCALE OF 1 TO 10
1 EQUALS VERY LOW
10 EQUALS VERY HIGH

RATING	DATE	TIME
_____	_____	_____
_____	_____	_____
_____	_____	_____

CAUSES OF LOW SELF-ESTEEM

There are many events and circumstances that can cause us to experience low self-esteem. Some are big things like losing a job. A divorce. A serious illness or disability. A financial setback. A temporary incarceration. A relationship gone wrong. Or the loss of a loved one.

Small things can also cause stress and affect our level of self-esteem. Things like personal disappointments, criticism, lack of recognition, the weather, extra work load, the TV news.

Most of these, of course, we have no control over. We can't dictate what the weather is going to be, how the stock market is going to perform or what will be read on this evening's TV nightly news.

It is true that we have little influence over our external environment, what happens around us. However, we have considerable control over our internal thoughts and feelings, what happens within us. We are in control of and responsible for our actions, attitudes and choices.

WHAT IS SELF-ESTEEM?

Synonyms of self-esteem include: self-respect, self-worth, self-regard, self-acceptance, self-satisfaction, self-confidence and self-love.

It is feeling worthy and able to meet life's challenges. It is liking ourselves and feeling competent about our ability to deal with adversity. It is as essential as the air we breathe and just as intangible. You will have it, lose it and be forced to rebuild it over and over again. It comes from the depth of our core, and is reflected in every single action that we take. It can impact our health, our job, our happiness, and our relationships with others.

ELEMENTS OF SELF-ESTEEM

The level of our self-confidence and self-esteem is determined by two key elements:

> 1. The degree to which we like ourselves and accept who we are, and
> 2. The degree to which we feel competent about our ability to deal with adversity.

Do you like yourself? Can you look in the mirror and say, I like you. Try it. This is not vanity. This is self-acceptance, a recognition of your self-worth.

Now, what's interesting and important about this is that you will like yourself **more** if you do **more** of those things that let you like yourself most—like being patient, controlling your temper, being helpful to others, completing a task, etc. and less of those things that cause you to like yourself least –like becoming angry, impatient, inconsiderate of others, and so forth.

Competence is the other key element of self-esteem. Your competence in dealing with a crisis situation, in adapting and responding to the unexpected, in overcoming and rebounding from adversity reveal a lot about your level of self-esteem in that moment.

COMMON CHARACTERISTICS

How do you recognize someone with low self-esteem? What are some of the common characteristics? People with low self-esteem lack self-confidence. Often they appear sad, depressed, angry or resentful. They look for and point out the faults in others. They're complainers and gossipers. They belittle and devalue other people. They try raising themselves up by putting others down.

What else do they do? Who do they blame when things go wrong? Society. The weather. Their boss. Their children. Their spouse. The neighbors. The government. Always someone else. They use sarcasm, teasing and fault-finding to embarrass and ridicule.

Do you know anyone like that? Are you sometimes like that yourself? It is quite easy to fall into this behavior. Among some groups, it is considered normal. And, if you don't go along with it, the gossiping and the tearing down of others, you become the target of the gossip and the criticism. People who do this are revealing that they have low self-esteem. They are insecure and full of self-doubt.

By contrast, people with high self-esteem are confident, congenial, happy, eager to help others, forgiving, patient, open-minded, willing to admit their mistakes and quick to give praise to others. They don't need to make others look bad to make themselves look good. When faced with adversity or disappointment, they accept it and use it as a learning experience rather than take it as a personal rejection. Are you sometimes like that? Which kind of person do you prefer to be? The choice is yours.

People who face serious adversities—financial or family crises, divorce, serious illness, a job in jeopardy, the death of a loved one—very often find their self-esteem being depleted. Perhaps you have experienced or are experiencing such an adversity right now. In the pages that follow, we're going to show you how you can rebound from that adversity and rebuild your self-esteem.

SELF-PORTRAIT AND SELF-TALK

For this next exercise, what I want you to do is identify a quality or characteristic of your personality that you feel best describes the kind of person that you think you are or describes your strongest personal trait. Have it begin with the same letter as the first letter of your first name. For example, "moody" Mary, "pessimistic" Patti, "cheerful" Charlie, etc.

Write it down on the Self Portrait page that follows. Next, write down four additional qualities or characteristics (these need not start with the same letter) that you feel best describe the kind of person that you are or describe important aspects of your personality. Write these down on the same page.

IF YOU THINK YOU CAN

SELF PORTRAIT

LIST ON THIS PAGE THE FIVE QUALITIES OR CHARACTERISTICS OF YOUR PERSONALITY THAT YOU BELIEVE BEST DESCRIBE YOU.

1. _____

2. _____

3. _____

4. _____

5. _____

Now, what do you say to yourself when things go wrong? Say that you misplace your wallet or purse and you're late for an appointment. You spill coffee or coke on yourself just before you are to make an important presentation. You trip over a step and fall. What do you say to yourself when this happens?

How embarrassed or angry do you become?

What do you say to yourself when you are faced with a new or difficult situation, like having to get up in front of a group for the very first time to make a presentation, or going on a job interview? Are you confident? Nervous? Scared?

Do you know what is the number 1 fear that most people have? Fear of public speaking. Even professional actors and performers admit to having butterflies just before a performance. Why? What are we afraid of? Being laughed at. Making a mistake. Giving a bad performance. Making a poor impression.

At times like these, is your self-talk positive or negative? What is it based on? Where do negative thoughts come from? Why do we have them? They have to do with and are directly related to our self-image, our self-portrait and our self-esteem. If we have a negative self-image, our thoughts will be negative. If we have a positive self-image, our thoughts will be positive.

Look back at the list of qualities or characteristics that you wrote down on the Self Portrait page. If you were totally honest with yourself, not all of those qualities were positive. And that's okay. Most everyone has a mix of pluses and minuses. What is important is that these descriptive qualities give us clues about how we feel about ourselves. It is true that these feelings can change from day-to-day, from moment-to-moment. But some do remain fairly constant, and this reveals our self-portrait. And from this self-portrait comes our self-talk. It is what we tell ourselves about our chances for success or failure when facing a situation. Based on what you wrote down, do you expect to succeed or fail when you try something new? Do you expect to be liked or rejected by other people when meeting them for the first time?

SELF CONCEPT

During one of the workshops I do, I hold up a crisp, new $20 bill and ask who in the audience would like it. Of course, everyone does. Then I crumple it up, pretend I spit on it, drop it on the floor and grind it with my heel. Picking it up all crumpled and dirty, I again ask the audience who would like to have it. And again, of course, everyone does.

Why is this so? Why are they willing to accept the dirty, crumpled, spit-upon $20 bill? Because, no matter what I did to it, it is still worth $20. It had not decreased in value.

Consider how we are like that $20 bill. Many times in our life our self-esteem, our self-confidence, will get crumpled, damaged, even ground into the dirt by circumstances, sometimes by our own actions or the decisions that we ourselves make. At those times, we may feel that we're worth a lot less. Right?

Rodney Dangerfield used to tell a lot of jokes on himself. He'd say things like: "I was such an ugly child that when I played in the sandbox, the cat kept covering me up." Rodney made a living at doing this, putting himself down. But unfortunately a lot of other people also make a practice of putting themselves down, and they don't get paid for it. Are you one of them?

I'm here to tell you that no matter what has happened to you in your life, or what may happen to you in the future, you have not lost your innate value as a human being. The worth of your life comes not from what others may think or say about you; it comes from what you believe about yourself.

THE FARMER'S DONKEY: A FABLE FOR OUR TIME
(Author unknown)

One day a farmer's donkey fell down into a well. The animal cried piteously for hours as the farmer tried to figure out what to do. Finally, he decided the animal was old and the well needed to be covered up anyway. It just wasn't worth it to retrieve the donkey. So, he invited all his neighbors to come over and help him.

They all grabbed shovels and began shoveling dirt into the well. At first, realizing what was happening, the donkey cried even louder. Then, to everyone's amazement, he quieted down.

A few shovel loads later, the farmer looked down the well and was astonished at what he saw. With every shovelful of dirt that hit his back, the donkey was doing something amazing. He was shaking it off and taking a step up. As the farmer's neighbors continued to shovel dirt on top of the animal, he continued to shake it off and take a step up. After a few more minutes, everyone stared in amazement as the donkey stepped up over the edge of the well and trotted off.

Life is going to shovel dirt on you, all kinds of dirt. The trick to getting out of the well is to shake it off and take a step up. We can see each of our troubles is a stepping stone. We can get out of the deepest well just by not stopping, never giving up, shaking it off and taking a step up!

ATTITUDES ABOUT FAILURE

Let's talk now about failure. How do you see failure? Is it a good thing or a bad thing? What were you told about failure by your parents? By your teachers? Some people can accept failure without fear, while others fear to fail.

Let's see if you can guess the name of this very famous man whose life was full of failures. He failed in business at 22. He ran for the Legislature and was defeated at 23. He failed again in business at 24. His sweetheart died when he was 26. He had a nervous breakdown at 27. He was defeated for Speaker of the House at 29. Defeated for Congress at 34. Defeated for Congress again at 39. Defeated for the Senate at 46. Defeated for Vice President at 47. Defeated again for the Senate at 49. Who was he?

Here's a hint. He was elected President of the United States at age 51, abolished slavery, was assassinated while president and has his picture on the $5 bill.

Abraham Lincoln, of course. Quite a failure! Wouldn't you say?

Here are some other good examples of failure: Babe Ruth, Thomas Edison, Walt Disney. Why do I call them failures? Well, Babe Ruth struck out twice as often as he hit a home-run. It took Thomas Edison 1000 attempts before he made a light bulb work, which means he failed 999 times. And Walt Disney was a school drop-out. A real bunch of failures, weren't they?

Yes, they were. But along with their failures, they also had some remarkable successes. How did they do it? What was their secret?

Persistance! They had persistence. They didn't give up. They kept on trying. There's an old Japanese proverb that says: (Nana korobi, ya oki.), It means fall down 7 times; stand up 8.

Beverly Sills, the famous opera star once said: You may be disappointed if you fail, but you are doomed if you don't try. The millionaire businessman R.H. Macy failed seven times before his store Macy's in New York caught on. English novelist John Creasey received 753 rejection letters before he published his 564 books. At age 67 Thomas Edison saw his laboratory completely destroyed by fire. Turning to a friend he said: "there is great value in disaster. All our mistakes are burned up." and then he went on to produce some of his greatest inventions. Entertainer/entrepreneur

Zig Ziglar put it this way: "If we learn from a defeat, we haven't really lost."

Another thing that helped Ruth, Edison and Disney succeed was practice. For them, failure was a form of practice — of discovering the wrong way to learn the right way. Practice and persistence are the path to success.

Failure is an integral part of the learning process, a stepping stone to success. No one ever learned to ride a horse, drive a car, play golf or speak a foreign language the very first time they tried. There is always a certain amount of mistake-making in learning a new skill. We can label it failure if we like. But by doing so, we are prejudicing our own ability to succeed. We are fixing in our minds an attitude of disappointment, a feeling of inadequacy, a sense of inferiority. If we should happen to luck out and do it right the first time, it may be impressive to others and very ego-satisfying to us, but it will not have taught us very much about how or why we succeeded. A little bit of failure, and what we learn, we learn well. I love the late comedian George Carlin's take on it. "If you try to fail, and succeed, which have you done?" So, should we fear failure or embrace it?

OVERCOMING ADVERSITY

A group of frogs were traveling through the woods one day when two of them fell into a deep pit. The other frogs gathered around the pit. When they saw how deep it was, they told the unfortunate frogs that they would never get out. The two frogs, at first, ignored the comments and tried to jump up out of the pit. The other frogs kept telling them to stop, that they were as good as dead.

Finally, one of the frogs took heed to what the other frogs were saying and gave up. He fell down and died. The other frog, however, continued to jump as hard as he could. Once again, the crowd of frogs yelled at him to stop the pain and suffering and just die. He jumped even harder and finally made it out.

When he got out, the other frogs asked him, "Why did you continue jumping? Didn't you hear us?" The frog explained that he was hard of hearing and he thought they were encouraging him the whole time.

What does this story teach us? There are two lessons. First, there is power of life and death in the tongue. An encouraging word to someone who is down can lift them up and help them make it through the day. A destructive word, on the other hand, to someone who is down can be devastating and can totally shatter their self-esteem. So, be careful of what you say to others and, even more importantly, be careful of how you say it.

Our tone of voice can send a very different message from the words we speak. Ninety percent of the friction in relationships between people is caused by using the wrong tone of voice. Listen to yourself and how you say things to your children, your friends, your spouse, your boss. Does your tone of voice convey irritation, annoyance or impatience? Or does it express eagerness, understanding and patience?

Try saying the word "No" in ten different ways, just by changing your tone of voice. Then do the same with the word "Yes." You will be amazed to discover that simply by changing your tone of voice you can communicate a sense of anger, fear, doubt, reluctance, agreement or joy. So, if you can do this with just one word, imagine how much more you are communicating through your tone of voice when you speak an entire sentence.

The second lesson from the story about the frogs is that what we say to ourselves when we're faced with criticism or failure is even more important than what people say to us. Do we say to ourselves words of encouragement or of discouragement? Do we believe that we are destined to succeed or doomed to fail? What did the second frog tell himself? It may be true that we can't always choose what happens to us, but we can choose what we do or say about it.

The good news is that the bad news can be changed to good news when we change our attitude. Life is ten percent what happens to us and ninety percent how we react to it.

YOUR ATTITUDE IS YOUR CHOICE

Attitude is more important than appearance. If you look unsure of yourself when you get up to give that presentation or go in for that job interview, it will show. And people will doubt your ability. If you look too serious or frown a lot, people will think you're unfriendly and stay away from you. On the other hand, if you have a positive attitude, you will attract new friends, get compliments from customers and receive favorable appraisals from your boss.

Attitude is more important than circumstance. It is more important than education, than money, than failure, than success. It is more important than what other people say or do. It is more important than our abilities or our skills. It will make or break a relationship, a home. It will determine how successful we are in getting a job and in keeping that job. It is in fact true that more people lose their jobs because they can't get along with the boss or their co-workers than because they can't do the job. "The single most important ingredient in the formula for success is knowing how to get along with people" (Teddy Roosevelt).

If you have a positive attitude and can get people to like you, they'll pretty much forgive you if you mess up. But if you have a bad attitude and are a grouch around your co-workers, they'll do everything they possibly can to get you fired.

The remarkable thing is that we have a choice every day about the attitude we carry with us during that day. We cannot change our past. But we can change our future — by our attitude in the present. We are in charge of our attitudes. To quote Oscar Wilde: "No man is rich enough to buy back his past, nor smart enough to foretell the future. But what we do have is the gift of the present."

If you feel you are unattractive, you can change it in an instant. Do you know how? With a smile. What is the most important thing you can wear when asking someone for a favor or going for a job interview? Your expression. So, remember, attitude is where it's at.

I know a man who is so negative that even when he has something positive to say, he puts it in a negative sentence. The other day, I invited him out to dinner. The food was fantastic, the service great, the décor very nice and the prices very reasonable. I asked for his comment.

"It's not a bad place." He said.

"But Tom," I protested. "The food, the service, the ambiance — Everything was wonderful, wasn't it?"

"That's what I said." He responded. "It's not a bad place."

What an attitude! What a way to live! What a shame to lose out on the opportunity to enjoy life.

SENTENCE COMPLETION EXERCISE

What I want you to do now is to complete three simple sentences that appear on the next two pages. Do so as quickly as possible. Don't take time to think about them. Write down the very first thing that comes to your mind. Be honest. This is going to help you to better understand your attitude and how you can change negative attitudes and build your self-confidence and self-esteem.

SENTENCE COMPLETION EXERCISE

AS QUICKLY AS POSSIBLE, WRITE FIVE ENDINGS TO EACH OF THE FOLLWING THREE STATEMENTS.

"I LIKE MYSELF MOST WHEN I ..."

1. _____
2. _____
3. _____
4. _____
5. _____

"I LIKE MYSELF LEAST WHEN I ..."

1. _____
2. _____
3. _____
4. _____
5. _____

IF YOU THINK YOU CAN

"IT'S NOT EASY FOR ME TO ADMIT THAT I ..."

1. _____

2. _____

3. _____

4. _____

5. _____

These are great admissions. They reveal how we truly feel about ourselves, what we like about ourselves, what we don't like about ourselves, what we think our strengths are as well as our weaknesses.

How can we change those aspects of our personality that we are not comfortable with? First, we must take ownership of our attitudes, actions and choices. We must stop blaming or crediting other people for how we feel. No one can make us feel bad, sad, angry, or happy. We decide how we feel. We may not be able to control circumstances or the actions of other people, but we can determine how we react to them.

And so, we can and should take credit for when things go well just as we can and should take responsibility for when they don't go so well. We are in charge. Read and affirm the statements on the following page, and believe that you are as British poet William Ernest Henley proudly proclaimed: "The Master of your fate, the Captain of your Soul."

TAKING OWNERSHIP OF OUR ACTIONS, ATTITUDES AND CHOICES

I AM RESPONSIBLE FOR …

- ☐ MY CHOICES AND MY ACTIONS

- ☐ THE WAY I PRIORITIZE MY TIME

- ☐ THE WAY I TREAT MY BODY

- ☐ THE WAY I CARE ABOUT MY JOB

- ☐ THE WAY I TREAT OTHER PEOPLE

- ☐ THE RELATIONSHIPS THAT I CHOOSE TO ENTER OR CHOOSE TO REMAIN IN

- ☐ MY HAPPINESS AND MY LIFE … MATERIALLY, EMOTIONALLY, INTELECTUALLY, SPIRITUALLY

I woke up early today, excited over all I get to do before the clock strikes midnight. My job is to choose what kind of day I am going to have. I can complain because it is raining or I can be thankful that the grass is getting watered for free.

I can grumble about having to go to school or to work or I can rejoice that I have a job or a school to go to. I can lament over all that my parents didn't give me when

I was growing up or I can feel grateful that they allowed me to be born.

I can cry because roses have thorns or I can celebrate that thorns have roses.

I can whine because I have to follow a healthy diet or I can shout for joy because, unlike millions of other people around the world, when I get home this evening, I will have something to eat.

Today stretches ahead of me, waiting to be shaped. And here I am, the sculptor who gets to do the shaping. What today will be like is up to me. I get to choose what kind of day I will have! Put simply, attitude is where it's at. And we are in charge of our attitude. We cannot change our past, but we can change our future — by our attitude in the present.

WISHED FOR QUALITIES

On the following page, I want you to make a Wish List. Choose three qualities you wish you had, that you admire in other people. They should be positive, personal characteristics like cheerful, loving, thoughtful, patient, friendly, a good talker, good money manager, etc. You pick them. Write them down, and underneath each, write down the name of the person you feel possesses that quality.

WISHED FOR QUALITIES

QUALITIES YOU WISH YOU HAD THAT YOU ADMIRE IN OTHER PEOPLE

QUALITY #1: _____

PERSON WHO HAS THIS QUALITY

_____

QUALITY #2: _____

PERSON WHO HAS THIS QUALITY

_____

QUALITY #3: _____

PERSON WHO HAS THIS QUALITY

_____

COMPLIMENT CIRCLE

Now, select a trusted friend or associate and pay him/her five sincere compliments, five positive qualities that you see in that individual. Then, ask him/her to give you five sincere compliments in return, five positive qualities that they see in you. Next, talk about how each of you felt being showered with these compliments.

Were you surprised by the compliments you received? Were you embarrassed? Why do we feel awkward or embarrassed when we are paid a compliment?

Is it because we feel people are lying to us?

Is it because we feel we don't deserve the compliments?

In our society we are taught that modesty is a virtue and that we should be suspicious of and reject all flattery. What happens when we turn down a compliment? Who does it hurt?

First of all, it hurts the person giving it, just as much as if we refused from them a bouquet of flowers or box of candy. By rejecting their compliment, we are questioning their motives or their judgment. We are also discouraging them from offering us any compliments in the future.

Secondly, it hurts us, because we miss out on the beauty and joy of receiving their gift. Compliments are an act of kindness. We often underestimate, undervalue our own positive qualities. Compliments are cool, and they nourish our self-esteem.

Which compliments were you able to accept from your friend most easily? Which were the hardest to accept?

Were any of the qualities seen in you by your friend on your Wish List? If so, go back and put a check mark next to that quality that others see in you, that you didn't know you had.

SELF-RATING EXERCISE

Turn back to the Self-Esteem Rating sheet on Page 11 and rate yourself once again, using the scale of 1 to 10. Write your rating and the time and date.

SIMPLE ACTS OF KINDNESS

What is an act of kindness? It can be as simple as a smile or a thoughtful phrase like Thank You. Have you performed an act of kindness today? Do you recall receiving one?

What about an act of kindness toward yourself? Have you given one to yourself today? Which feels better? Which do you prefer? Which does us more good?

Certainly doing something nice for ourselves feels good. What about when we do something nice for someone else? How does it make us feel? Important. Significant. Worthwhile.

Why are acts of kindness important? They are important because they make us feel valued. They raise our self-esteem. And, in a much larger sense, there is less suffering in the world each time someone performs a random act of kindness. "My religion is kindness" (Dalai Lama).

To help you become aware of the many acts of kindness which surround your life, I want you to start a Daily Journal beginning today and continue with it for 15 days. You are to list acts of kindness done to you, and acts of kindness you do for others. Your goal is to perform and record at least three acts of kindness each day. On the following Pages, there is a Daily Journal for you to make your entries.

ACTS OF KINDNESS DAILY JOURNAL
WEEK ONE

SUNDAY - ACTS OF KINDNESS DONE BY YOU

1. _____

2. _____

3. _____

ACTS OF KINDNESS RECEIVED FROM OTHERS

1. _____

2. _____

3. _____

MONDAY - ACTS OF KINDNESS DONE BY YOU

1. _____

2. _____

3. _____

ACTS OF KINDNESS RECEIVED FROM OTHERS

1. _____

2. _____

3. _____

TUESDAY - ACTS OF KINDNESS DONE BY YOU

1. _____

2. _____

3. _____

ACTS OF KINDNESS RECEIVED FROM OTHERS

1. _____

2. _____

3. _____

WEDNESDAY - ACTS OF KINDNESS DONE BY YOU

1. _____

2. _____

3. _____

ACTS OF KINDNESS RECEIVED FROM OTHERS

1. _____

2. _____

3. _____

THURSDAY - ACTS OF KINDNESS DONE BY YOU

1. _____

2. _____

3. _____

ACTS OF KINDNESS RECEIVED FROM OTHERS

1. _____

2. _____

3. _____

FRIDAY - ACTS OF KINDNESS DONE BY YOU

1. _____

2. _____

3. _____

ACTS OF KINDNESS RECEIVED FROM OTHERS

1. _____

2. _____

3. _____

SATURDAY – ACTS OF KINDNESS DONE BY YOU

1. _____

2. _____

3. _____

ACTS OF KINDNESS RECEIVED FROM OTHERS

1. _____

2. _____

3. _____

ACTS OF KINDNESS DAILY JOURNAL
WEEK TWO

SUNDAY - ACTS OF KINDNESS DONE BY YOU
1. _____
2. _____
3. _____

ACTS OF KINDNESS RECEIVED FROM OTHERS
1. _____
2. _____
3. _____

MONDAY - ACTS OF KINDNESS DONE BY YOU
1. _____
2. _____
3. _____

ACTS OF KINDNESS RECEIVED FROM OTHERS
1. _____
2. _____
3. _____

TUESDAY - ACTS OF KINDNESS DONE BY YOU

1. _____

2. _____

3. _____

ACTS OF KINDNESS RECEIVED FROM OTHERS

1. _____

2. _____

3. _____

WEDNESDAY - ACTS OF KINDNESS DONE BY YOU

1. _____

2. _____

3. _____

ACTS OF KINDNESS RECEIVED FROM OTHERS

1. _____

2. _____

3. _____

THURSDAY - ACTS OF KINDNESS DONE BY YOU

1. _____

2. _____

3. _____

ACTS OF KINDNESS RECEIVED FROM OTHERS

1. _____

2. _____

3. _____

FRIDAY - ACTS OF KINDNESS DONE BY YOU

1. _____

2. _____

3. _____

ACTS OF KINDNESS RECEIVED FROM OTHERS

1. _____

2. _____

3. _____

SATURDAY – ACTS OF KINDNESS DONE BY YOU

1. _____

2. _____

3. _____

ACTS OF KINDNESS RECEIVED FROM OTHERS

1. _____

2. _____

3. _____

Now, go back and read over the sequence of events, experiences and verbal exchanges that you recorded throughout the past two weeks. It will surprise and reassure you that there is still much kindness in the world. Despite the media's emphasis on negative news, simple and extraordinary acts of kindness by ordinary people occur every day.

Recently I was in Washington DC making the rounds of the Capitol for an organization I belong to. We visited with staff of 28 U.S. Congressional representatives in one day. Extremely hectic. Our last appointment concluded at 6:00 PM.

Exiting the Rayburn Building, we tried to find a taxi to take us back to our hotel. But several hundred other people had the same idea. Then it started to rain. We called a couple of local cab companies, who informed us that no taxis were available. The rain turned to icy sleet. Cold, wet and discouraged we went back inside the building to wait. An hour and a half later, we were still waiting, and the weather was worsening. What to do?

Then, unexpectedly, a well-dressed gentleman in his mid 30's, approached us and asked where we were going. We told him the name of the hotel and how long we had been waiting for a taxi. He said he would take us there.

Astonished, we gratefully accepted. On the drive to our hotel, we learned that he was the General Chef and Manager over all the cafeterias and private dining-rooms for the three Congressional office buildings.

He took time away from his job to help out three cold, wet and weary strangers. An incredible act of kindness — and one that we will not soon forget.

Likewise, I have no doubt that that young man will long remember the incident as well, and that he felt a deep sense of personal satisfaction and fulfillment knowing that he was able to unselfishly serve three fellow human beings. For it is in serving others that we experience the greatest joy and elevate our human worth. "What do we live for if not to make life less difficult for each other" (George Eliot).

MOLDING OUR IMAGE

For this next exercise you will need a ball of clay.

What I want you to do with the ball of clay is to model it into whatever you want in just 30 seconds time. Next, give it to a family member or friend and ask them to model it into whatever shape they choose, again in just 30 seconds. Next, give it to a third person and ask that they do the same. Now examine the ball of clay and notice how different it is from its original shape and even from the shape into which you modeled it.

How are we like the ball of clay? We are molded or changed by many things — by other people, by our parents, our spouses, the environment, economic conditions, illness, etc. Are you the same person you were last year? No. What about yesterday? Will you be the same person tomorrow? Definitely not.

Some things we have control over. Others we do not. If you hold yourself responsible for those things beyond your control, you put your self-esteem in jeopardy, because inevitably you will fail your expectations. Likewise if you deny responsibility for those things within your control, you are also jeopardizing your self-esteem. You are relinquishing control to someone else.

Circumstances can and do influence our opinions of ourselves, our self-confidence and self-esteem. But we can control how much they influence us. Remember what we said in earlier pages. You can't always choose what happens to you, but you can choose how you react to it.

WHAT IS RESILIENCY?

Resiliency is the ability to bounce back after being knocked down by disappointment, rejection, loss, failure or injury. Resiliency is the key to regaining and rebuilding our self-esteem.

If you take that same ball of clay and throw it on the floor what happens to it? Two things: It takes on a different shape, and it stays on the floor. If, instead, you throw a rubber ball on the floor what happens?

It doesn't change its shape or stay on the floor. It bounces back. This is called resiliency. Resiliency lets us bounce back from a situation, retain our shape like the rubber ball or renew ourselves like plants that hibernate during the winter and then bloom again in the spring.

If you stub your toe, it's okay to say ouch! and nurse the hurt for a bit. But if it was a year ago that you did it, it's time to put your shoe back on and go for a walk.

Adversity and failure can be hard to take sometimes. They can deliver a crushing blow to your self-esteem, and you may not always know how to recover or rebound. So, I'm going to give you seven simple strategies to follow that will help you rebound from adversity, disappointment, failure, a hostile personal encounter with someone or a loss of some kind. Here is what you do.

RESILIENCY SKILLS

1. **Step back**. Step back from the problem. Take a time-out. Put some distance, physical and emotional distance, between yourself and the person or situation that's causing you the stress. Give yourself the necessary time and space to think about it calmly. In most cases, you don't need to rush into making a hasty decision. In fact, in some instances, doing so can be the wrong thing to do. So, take the time you need to think about all the various choices and how you want to respond. The amount of time you need to calmly and thoughtfully consider your options will depend on each situation.

If you are in a situation where it is difficult for you to physically distance yourself from the problem, temporarily close your mind to the external environment by emotionally detaching yourself from it and mentally focusing on images of happier times and places. POW's have found this technique helped them survive long periods of incarceration.

2. **Hug yourself**. – mentally and verbally. Tell yourself that you are a good person—because you are. Remind yourself of your past accomplishments. Recognize and appreciate your positive qualities, your talents, your abilities. Give yourself credit for all that you have done for your family, your friends, for strangers. To quote actress Jennifer Anison from the book: The Right Words at the Right Times by Marlo Thomas: "We need to celebrate who we are and what we have to give to the world." We do not acknowledge enough the good that we have done, the achievements we have made, the contributions, small and large, that we have given to others during our life times. When we are hurting because of a loss, a disappointment or other adversity, it is appropriate that we soothe our pain and nourish our spirit with the balm of self-praise and positive reflection.

3. **Smile**. Find the humor in the situation. There always is. Be willing to laugh at yourself and your mistakes.

Here's a little story that came to me across the Internet not long ago. A young man walks his girl home after their first date. Inspired by the full moon, he decides to ask her for a good-night kiss. Leaning his hand against the wall, he says, "Hey baby, how 'bout a goodnight kiss?"

She protests. "My parents will see us!"

"Oh come on," he says. "There's nobody around, they're all sleeping!"

"No. It's too risky!"
"Please, please, I like you so much!!"
"I like you too, but I just can't!" she responds.
"Say yes, please." He begs.

Suddenly the porch light goes on, and the girl's sister shows up in her pajamas, hair disheveled. The sister says: "Dad says to go ahead and give him a kiss. Or I can do it. Or if need be, he'll come down himself and do it. But for crying out loud tell him to take his hand off the intercom button!"

Humor can help heal the hurt caused by disappointment, rejection or failure. Laughter definitely is good medicine.

4. **Forgive**. Forgive those who have wronged you. Since we can't possibly know what problems or difficulties the person who wronged us might have been facing at the time, how certain can we be that their intentions to harm us were deliberate?

Several years ago I read an article about a group of Tibetan monks in San Francisco who had spent months creating a mandala (an elaborate geometric design symbolizing the universe) for the museum, which was then senselessly destroyed in a matter of seconds by an emotionally disturbed woman. Their astonishing response to the destruction of their mandala was — total forgiveness, love and compassion toward the perpetrator. When asked how they could be so forgiving, the Tibetan monks replied: "We don't know how to judge her motivation. We cannot know what was in her mind or in her heart."

And, even if the wrong to us was deliberate, we can choose to express our forgiveness and a sincere personal wish for happiness and success for our critics, our enemies and for all humankind. Forgiveness allows us to unburden ourselves of our anger and resentment which are deeply harmful to us physically as well as spiritually.

If the mistake was ours, we must forgive ourselves. This is often the hardest thing to do. Remember we are not perfect, and we are not expected to be perfect. Forgive yourself for whatever mistake you made yesterday and choose to act tomorrow with the wisdom you have gained.

5. **Analyze.** Analyze your situation and your goals. Examine all of the options. Go outside of the box and look for creative, nontraditional solutions.

Here is a simple exercise that can help you do that. On a sheet of blank paper, make nine dots. Three rows of three dots each, as shown to the left. Now, connect all of the dots by drawing just four lines, without lifting your pen from the paper.

After you have tried, turn to the next page to see how it can be done. Don't peak.

"Oh, but wait, you didn't say I could go out of the nine dots." You protest.

I didn't say that you couldn't either. You put the restriction on yourself. And that's the point. By doing so, you limited your choices and the possible solutions to the problem.

Listen also to your intuition. Intuition is instinctive knowing based on conscious experience and subconscious knowledge. Many CEO's have admitted to trusting their intuition when making some of their most critical corporate decisions.

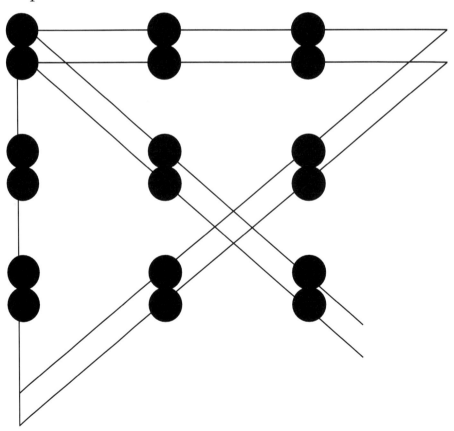

6. **Take charge**. Assert control over your problem. Make a decision. Don't wait for someone else to make it for you, and don't agonize over whether it's the right decision. Trust yourself that it is the best decision you can possibly make for that time and that situation. Nothing is forever, and nothing is absolute. You can, if you need to, change your decision in the future, if circumstances change or you receive new information.

7. **Go forward**. Now, go forward with your decision with confidence and conviction. Believe that you have made the best possible decision you could, because you have, for that moment in time.

To review, the seven strategies for dealing with adversity are: Step back, Hug yourself, Smile, Forgive, Analyze, Take charge and Go forward.

You may not follow all of these steps in every situation. But by being aware of their power, you can choose how to react to every circumstance.

Years ago a man in his 60's was offered $200,000 for a restaurant-motel-service station business that he'd spent his life building up. He turned the offer down, because he loved the business and wasn't ready to retire yet. Two years later, at 65, he was flat broke with no income to look forward to but a small Social Security check each month. The state had built a new highway bypassing his business and he lost it.

Most people would have been crushed by such a blow, but this man refused to give up. Instead, he took stock. There was one thing he knew how to do—fry chicken. Maybe he could sell that knowledge to others. He kissed his wife good-bye and, in a battered old car with a pressure cooker and a can of specially prepared flour, set out to sell his idea to other restaurants. It was tough going, and he often slept in the car because there wasn't enough money for a hotel room. But a few years later, he had built a nationwide franchised restaurant chain. The man was Colonel Sanders and his now famous chain of restaurants is Kentucky Fried Chicken.

SHARED EXPERIENCES

What about you? Can you remember a time when you bounced back from failure or adversity—a time when you tried a little harder and succeeded. It might have been in school, playing a sport, dealing with an illness, a job assignment, whatever. What made you successful?

As mentioned earlier, one of the keys to success is practice. Learning from our mistakes, like Tom Edison. Another key is to ask questions of people who know more than we do. This is called "networking" or tapping into resources. And the third key is persistence, refusing to give up.

Here are a couple more quotes. Mary Kay, the cosmetics queen once said: "One of the secrets of success is to refuse to let temporary setbacks defeat us." And this from Helen Keller, "The marvelous richness of human experience would lose something of rewarding joy if there were not limitations to overcome." What she was saying was that adversity makes our successes even sweeter. "The greater the obstacle, the more glory in overcoming it" (Moliere).

So, which do you prefer to be — the rubber ball or the ball of clay? You have a choice. You can fall down after the first punch and stay down for the count or you can bounce back up and keep on fighting.

PART 2: FULFILLING YOUR DREAMS

DREAM GOALS

If I only had— Have you ever said that to yourself? If I only had a better job, better looks, better health, better support from my family—I would be a better person. Right?

The next page is titled "Dream Goals." What I want you to do is choose two Dream Goals you wish you could have. Common goals like: money, good health, a good job, spiritual peace, respect, happiness, better appearance, better family relationships, more friends, a better education whatever you like. Go inside and ask yourself: What do I really want?

Now, there is a difference between a "dream" and a "Dream Goal." A dream is something you fantasize about, wish for and hope to have come true—like the young, single mother who desperately wanted to win the lottery and prayed for it to happen, but it didn't. Then one day, she lost her job, and that night she knelt down and prayed more fervently to God to please let her win the lottery. Still nothing happened. The next day, her house caught on fire and burned to the ground. Now, totally distraught and desperate, she once again knelt down and prayed for God to let her win the lottery. There was a flash of lightning and a roll of thunder, and a voice from above spoke: "Maria, I hear your prayer to win the lottery. But Maria, you've got to do your part. You've got to buy a ticket."

A Dream Goal is something you're serious about, something you plan for, something you are committed to and are willing to work for.

So, write down your two top Dream Goals. Be very specific. If money is one of your Dream Goals, write down how much you would want. If your Dream Goal is to have a different job, define the kind of job you would want it to be. If your goal is to lose a few inches around your waist, excellent but get specific. If your goal is to go back to school, fine. Which school and what would you want to study?

Next, set a date by when you want to achieve each of these Dream Goals. Again, be specific. Don't write down "In about 5 years." Write down a specific calendar date.

DREAM GOALS

GOAL #1: _____
TARGET DATE: _____

    STEP 1:

    STEP 2:

    STEP 3:

GOAL #2: _____
TARGET DATE: _____

    STEP 1:

    STEP 2:

    STEP 3:

FROM DREAM TO REALITY

How can you make your Dream Goals become reality? First, you must be truly committed to them. You must really, really want them. You have to be willing to make sacrifices for them. You have to be willing to put in time and effort to accomplish them. Do you feel that way about each of your Dream Goals?

Are you committed? You may be involved with them but are you truly committed to them? Let me explain the difference between being committed and just being involved. Think about your morning breakfast of a plate of bacon and eggs. Now, the chicken was involved, but the pig was truly committed.

So, are you committed?

Before we go on, do you want to change any of your Dream Goals? It's okay to do that. Goals and priorities can and do change, just as we change and as circumstances change.

If these then are the Dream Goals you are committed to today, how can you make them become reality? The first thing is to be sure that they are very specific, clearly stated. If you're planning a trip, you have to decide what your destination is. Otherwise, when you get there, you won't know you've arrived.

Second, you have to have a specific date. By when do you want to achieve your Dream Goal? Imagine if you called up an airline to book a flight to Chicago and when the reservation agent asked you when you wanted to arrive, you'd tell them "Oh, sometime this year." That won't work. You need to select the date and the time, even if later you have to change your schedule. Having a target date keeps you focused on your Dream Goal.

As an example, let's say you want to begin exercising regularly. An excellent goal if you chose it as one of yours. Not everyone, however, likes to exercise. When I suggested a daily exercise routine to a friend, she said, "If God meant for us to touch our toes, he would have put 'em a lot closer to our knees."

Okay, what you do next is divide your Dream Goal into smaller goals or steps, as shown on the Dream Goal page. The idea is to make it easy for you to be successful. And so, if one of your Dream Goals is to start exercising regularly, what might Step 1 be?

Join a health club? Perhaps. Maybe first you need to decide what kind of exercise you want to do. Jogging? Swimming? Bicycling? Weight-lifting? Walking? Racquetball? Tennis? Working cross-word puzzles? Well, the cross-word puzzles may be fun and a good mental exercise, but they're not going to do much for your waistline.

Whatever exercise you choose, you need to be specific. And you want to pick an exercise that you will truly enjoy. Because if you don't enjoy it, you won't stay with it.

After you decide on the exercise you're going to practice, your next step is to decide whether you will prefer to exercise alone or with a family member or friend. It can help to have a friend or partner to exercise with. But be sure that the partner you pick is equally committed and equally enthusiastic. Otherwise, they may wind up demotivating you and causing you to quit.

Depending on what exercise you choose, you will need to figure out where you are going to do it. Will it be indoors? Outdoors? At home? At a health club? If outdoors, how will the weather affect your plans? If at a health club, how much is it going to cost? Can your budget handle the extra expense?

So now you've chosen the exercise, a partner and where you're going to do it. What's next? You need to decide how often. How many times a week and at what time of day? One friend of mine told me his plan was to exercise very early in the morning before his brain figured out what he was doing.

Your final step is to decide when you will begin and for how many weeks you're going to keep it up. Make it easy on yourself. I suggest you set a goal of say six weeks to begin with. You want to make your first goal doable and not too far away, so that you can reward yourself when you achieve it. Yes, reward yourself. That's very important. Plan on doing something nice for yourself when you reach your goal. Take yourself to the movies. Have a meal at your favorite restaurant. Buy that special music CD or DVD you've been wanting. You deserve it.

Then, set a goal for another six weeks or three months. And when you achieve that goal, give yourself another reward. Before you know it, you will have been exercising for an entire year and feeling a whole lot better about yourself.

Let's take another goal. Let's say, one of your Dream Goals is to get a different job. That's not uncommon. Most people don't pick their jobs. They let their jobs pick them. That's why, according to human resources professionals, 80% of people working today are in the wrong jobs either because they are not happy there or because they are not fully utilizing their talents and abilities.

Okay, what might be Step 1? First you must decide where you want to work and for whom? That's right. You decide on the kind of job you would most like to have and where you want to work.

Do you want to work in a small office? For a large corporation? In a school? A store? In a job where you have contact with a lot of people? Or one where you work mainly with machines or computers? Do you want to move to another city? You need to ask yourself and answer all of these questions before you begin your job search.

Sit down and write out a one-page description of what would be the perfect job for you. Be very detailed. See yourself doing that job and describe a typical day — your duties, responsibilities and the work environment. Next, using the Internet or the library, find out what companies have jobs closest to the one you have described as your perfect job. Make a list.

Next, contact these companies by telephone, by mail or via the Internet to find out what specific skills and qualifications are required for the jobs you are interested in. They will be happy to tell you.

Now, ask yourself if you presently have these skills. If not, that's okay. It simply means you need to set a new goal of upgrading your skills and qualifications to be competitive for that job. Perhaps it means you need to go back to school. Take a few classes in computer technology, customer service, accounting or auto mechanics. Maybe you need to complete that college degree you gave up on five years ago. Whatever it takes.

If you really, really want that perfect job, you have to be ready to put in the time and effort to get it. Important career goals and job changes don't come easily or happen quickly. Remember Abraham Lincoln. How many times did he fail?

Your Dream Goal might be to get out of debt, buy your first house, travel to Europe, quit smoking, learn a foreign language or start your own business. Whatever it is, I can assure you, it is achievable. It is possible that it may not be achievable right away or in the specific time frame that you want it to be. But, you can achieve it. Yes, you might need to be flexible, to modify the target date. And that's okay, because you are not giving up your Dream Goal, you are simply adjusting to circumstance.

So, if you are patient enough, dedicated enough, willing to sacrifice enough, be assured that you can attain your Dream Goals, whatever they happen to be.

Setting Yourself Up For Success!

Do you think that success is a matter of luck?

If not luck then what? What do you think brings success?

Success does not happen by accident. It takes effort, practice and careful planning. Some people fail to achieve their goals, not because their goals are unattainable, but because they don't plan or prepare themselves well enough or because they shoot too high too early. An Olympic gold medalist first has to compete and win in his own home town before taking part in the world games.

Take it slow. Ask yourself to achieve reasonable goals, small goals at first. By making your small goals stepping stones toward your big goals, you can experience and enjoy being successful along the way. Confidence gained from successfully accomplishing these minigoals will energize and motivate you toward achieving your next set of minigoals and eventually your main goal. Success breeds success. And confidence gained from a successful experience will generate more confidence. And increased confidence and success in one area will motivate you to improve your skills in other areas, thus increasing your overall success and self-esteem.

Always remember, it's important to reward yourself and to make pursuing your Dream Goals fun. If the journey isn't enjoyable, you're not likely to complete the trip.

A POOR FARM GIRL

Let me now tell you a story about a poor farm girl from Delaware. At age 16, she dropped out of high school to help support her parents and siblings. She got married and had three children. But her husband died and she became a widow at age 32. With no money and no skills, she was left a single parent with a family to raise. To keep from going on welfare, she worked two jobs. One of them was as a lowly clerk in the Delaware State House of Representatives. Next, she got a job as receptionist in the governor's office where she developed a keen interest in government and politics. She returned to school, earned her GED and went on to College. In 1974 she decided to run for public office. She became a candidate for state representative and was elected. She got re-elected three more times. Then, in 1982 she ran for the state senate and was elected, serving for ten years until 1992. During that time, she built a successful family business with her second husband. Unfortunately he died of cancer in 1991 making her a widow for a second time. In 1993, she won the race for Lieutenant Governor. She won again in 1997. And in 2001, Mrs. Ruth Ann Minner became the first woman governor of the state of Delaware. She was re-elected to a 2nd term in 2005. A pretty remarkable journey for a poor girl from down on the farm, and a true testament to what can be accomplished through commitment, dedication and determination.

Success is getting up just one more time than you fall down. Remember the Japanese saying *(Nana korobi, ya oki.)*, *Fall down 7 times; stand up 8*. A successful person is one who can lay a firm foundation with the bricks that others throw at him. Henry Ford said it this way: "Whether you think you can or whether you think you can't, you are right."

CONTINGENCY PLANS.

Another important key to success is to have a contingency plan. Things don't always go as smoothly as we would want or expect. Let's say, for example, your neighbor promises to give you a ride to school so that you can take an evening computer class, and then tells you at the last minute they can't. You need to have a backup plan. Be prepared. Don't waste time bemoaning your bad luck. Do something about it. Practice the Seven Strategies of Resiliency and learn this little tongue-twister: Proper prior planning prevents poor performance. And, be flexible.

AGE IS NO EXCUSE

Age is no excuse and no obstacle to achieving your Dream Goals. Here is another story. This one is about a little old lady who is blind, 82 years old and power lifts 220 lbs! Not long ago she won her 175th gold medal and was inducted into Canada's Terry Fox Hall of Fame. Her name is Sarah Thompson. She's known as "supergranny." She's been competing since she was 62. At 65 she was running the 100 yard dash in 16 seconds and power lifting 250 lbs.

You're never too old to pursue a dream. Golda Meir was 71 when she became Prime Minister of Israel. Ben Franklin was 81 when he helped frame our constitution. George Bernard Shaw was 94 when one of his plays was first produced on Broadway. George Burns was in his 90's and still starring in Hollywood movies.

There are three kinds of people in the world: those who watch what's happening, those who wonder what's happening and those who make it happen. Which kind do you want to be? Why not make that a goal? Don't wait. Remember, in just two days, tomorrow will be yesterday.

BE PROUD OF WHO YOU ARE

Yes, be proud of who you are. I want you to become aware that there are many goals that you have already accomplished and that you will accomplish for which you should feel proud. Take a few moments now to reflect back on all that you have already done. On the next page, make a list of at least ten past accomplishments – small ones, big ones. It doesn't matter. You did them.

We don't give ourselves enough credit, enough recognition for our achievements, for goals we have already attained – completed school, raised a family, survived an accident, a disability, a divorce. Lots of things for which we can and should feel justly proud. Yes, it's okay to pat yourself on the back. In fact, it's healthy to do so. Recognizing all that we have done gives us the courage and the confidence to do more, to face new challenges and to succeed.

REFLECT BACK ON YOUR LIFE AND ALL THAT YOU HAVE ACHIEVED AND LIST TEN PERSONAL ACCOMPLISHMENTS

1. _____
2. _____
3. _____
4. _____
5. _____
6. _____
7. _____
8. _____
9. _____
10. _____

BEING YOUR OWN JUDGE

Who decides if you are a success or a failure? You do.

Who decides if you should give up? You do.

Remember, the worth of our lives comes not from what others may think or say about us, but from what we believe about ourselves. It's a question of perspective.

What is beauty in the eyes of a toad? "A female with two pop eyes, a wide mouth, yellow belly and spotted back" (Voltaire). Beauty is in the eye of the beholder. And so are success and failure.

A pessimist is someone who makes difficulties of his/her opportunities. An optimist is someone who makes opportunities of his/her difficulties. Which do you choose to be?

Success and happiness are not matters of chance but matters of choice.

AFFIRMATION OF PRIDE

This next exercise is very, very important. It is a powerful Affirmation of Pride. Read the statements that appear on the next page, out loud, standing in front of a mirror, every day, for 30 days.

AFFIRMATION OF PRIDE

READ THESE STATEMENTS BELOW
OUT LOUD EACH DAY, STANDING IN FRONT
OF A MIRROR FOR 30 DAYS

****

I BELIEVE IN ME!

I AM PROUD OF WHO I AM.

I AM PROUD OF WHAT I HAVE DONE.

I AM PROUD OF WHAT I WILL BECOME.

I BELIEVE IN ME!

If you will faithfully say these Affirmations daily, out loud, for one month, you will notice a difference — a positive difference, a change in your attitude, a change in your life, and good things will start to happen.

SELF-ESTEEM RATING EXERCISE

Turn now back to the Self-Esteem Rating sheet on page 11. I want you to rate yourself one more time. How do you feel about yourself right now, on that scale of 1 to 10? Write down your rating. Has your rating changed from the other two entries? It is quite natural that it would. Our self-esteem ebbs and flows like the ocean tides. But now you know that you can influence just how high or how low it goes.

POINTS TO REMEMBER

Let us review some of the ideas we have talked about in these pages.

1. Failure is not a dirty word. It is a way to learn.
2. Our attitude is our choice. We can't always choose what happens to us, but we can choose how we react to it.
3. People with low self-esteem put others down.
4. People with high self-esteem accept disappointments and use them as a learning experience.
5. Compliments are cool. They help nourish our self-esteem.

6. Doing acts of kindness for others makes us feel good about ourselves and raises our self-esteem.
7. Our true worth comes not from what others may think or say about us, but from what we believe about ourselves.
8. It is better to be a rubber ball than a lump of clay.
9. The Seven Strategies of resiliency that can help us retain or regain our self-esteem are to: Step back; Give ourselves a hug; Smile; Forgive ourselves and our critics; Analyze the problem; Take charge of the problem; and Go forward.
10. We can turn our "Dream Goals" into reality through careful planning, patience and persistence.
11. While you're doing all this, you are repeating to yourself the Affirmation of Pride, "I believe in me."

Is this hard to do? Yes, it can be, because we are used to our old habits, our old beliefs, our old way of thinking.

There are two rules for achieving anything.

Rule 1: Get started. And…

Rule 2: Keep going.

Let me share with you a beautiful poem called "Life's Lessons From A Butterfly." It's one of my favorites. The author is anonymous. Its message, no pun intended, is truly uplifting.

Let go of the past;
Trust the future;
Embrace change;
Come out of the cocoon;
Unfurl your wings;
Dare to get off the ground;
Ride on the breezes; Savor all the flowers;
Put on your brightest colors;
And soar high with your golden dreams.

THE CHEROKEE CHIEF

An old Cherokee Indian was teaching his grandson about life. "A fight is going on inside me," he said. It is a terrible fight and it is between two wolves. One is evil. He is anger, envy, sorrow, regret, greed, arrogance, self-pity, guilt, resentment, inferiority, lies, false pride, superiority, and ego. The other is good. He is joy, peace, love, hope, serenity, humility, kindness, benevolence, empathy, generosity, truth, compassion, and faith. This same fight is going on inside you - and inside every other person, too."

The grandson thought for a minute and then asked: "And grandfather, which wolf is going to win?"

The old Cherokee replied, "The one you feed."

And so it is. The choice is yours. Eleanor Roosevelt, wife of the late President Franklin D. Roosevelt, said: "The future belongs to those who believe in the beauty of their dreams."

Happiness doesn't depend on how much you have to enjoy but how much you enjoy what you have. Plenty of people miss out on their share of happiness not because they never found it, but because they didn't stop to enjoy it.

The Diary of Ann Frank recounts the extraordinary story of a young Jewish girl and her family during World War II under Hitler's Nazi occupation of her country. Despite the terrible ordeal that she endured, she was able to express a powerful an amazingly optimistic message for us to learn from. She wrote: "Everyone has inside him/her a piece of good news. The good news is that you don't yet realize how great you can be. How much you can love. What you can accomplish. And what your potential is."

I encourage you to believe in your dreams, believe in yourself and believe that the best for you is yet to be.

You can, if you think you can, rebound from adversity, discover the great potential within you and fulfill your most cherished dreams.

SUGGESTED READINGS

Branden, Nathaniel
   "The Power Of Self-Esteem"
   (Barnes & Noble Book, 1992)

Branden, Nathaniel
   "The Six Pillars Of Self-Esteem"
   (Bantom Books, 1993)

Coopersmith, Stanley
   "The Antecedents Of Self-Esteem, 2nd Ed."
   (Consulting Psychologists Pr. Inc., 1981)

Dyer, Wayne W.
   "10 Secrets For Success And Inner Peace"
   (Hay House, Inc. 2001)

Gulley, Philip
   "Front Porch Tales"
   (HarperOne, 2001)

James, William
   "Principles Of Psychology"
   (Harvard University Press, 1983)

Thomas, Marlo and Friends
   "The Right Words at the Right Times"
   (Atria Books, 2002)

Wollen, Steven & Cybil
   "The Resilient Self"
   (Randomhouse, 1993)

Made in the USA
Lexington, KY
16 September 2018